The Diary of Roy and Hayley Cropper

An unofficial Coronation Street companion book

With a foreword by Julie Hesmondhalgh

Glenda Young

THE DIARY OF ROY AND HAYLEY CROPPER

An unofficial Coronation Street companion book

First published as A Perfect Duet by FBS Publishing in 2014

Text copyright: Glenda Young

Cover design: Jo Blakeley

Foreword

By Julie Hesmondhalgh

What a treat this lovely little book is! I cannot lie, it was a bit emotional reading through it: reliving, in brief, sixteen of the happiest years of my life, namely those spent playing Hayley, in partnership with the great David Neilson as Roy.

And there is so much I'd forgotten! Ida Clough, Janice nicking a pan off the back of our first wedding car to bash Les with Stuart the builder who set Hayley's heart a flutter before he found out about her past and turned … And I can't believe how many thousands of pounds the poor Croppers shelled out over the years to various miscreants (and usually to buy children from them!)

And running alongside Hayley and Roy's story, as I read, I'm aware of the real events of my own life unfolding too. The *Weatherfield Gazette* reporter sent by Les to ruin the Croppers' church blessing in 1999 ended up being my real-life husband, Ian Kershaw. Hayley's spell in prison after 'kidnapping' Wayne covered my time off to have my first baby, Auntie Monica's illness (during which Roy had his fateful non-night with Tracy) enabled a sabbatical to go travelling before Martha started school, and Mrs Cropper's African adventure meant a year at home with my second daughter.

So many happy memories of wonderful times with wonderful actors: all my factory girl friends over the years (and Sean!), speaking and non-speaking, the gorgeous Kate Ford so brilliantly playing Tracy, Hayley's only enemy, Alma, Anna, Carla, Mary, Linda, Alison, Becky, Fiz ... all those unlikely but beautiful friendships, on and off screen. And it goes without saying that my friendships with those behind the scenes: the amazing crew, production team, writers, directors, make up girls, will live on too, long after Hayley is forgotten.

Thank you, Glenda, for this brisk, thorough and heartfelt celebration of a partnership I was so very lucky to have been part of for such a long period of my life (I was 27 when Hayley had that first dinner at Alma's with Curly, Audrey, and of course Roy!) I will treasure it as a prized memento of sixteen years in the best show in the world, sharing the screen with one of the finest actors I'll ever work with: my friend David Neilson.

And a huge thank you to all the Corrie fans for holding the Croppers in such a special place in your hearts for all these years. Look after Roy for me!

With my love and best wishes,

Julie Hesmondhalgh xx March 2014

1998

Hayley Ann Patterson meets Royston Cropper

Hayley Patterson arrived on Coronation Street in January 1998. We first see her in Curly's office at Firman's Freezers where he's giving her a rollicking for not being assertive enough with the other staff.

Hayley is befriended at work by Alma, who soon starts to wonder if her new colleague might be a bit too lonely for her own good after she receives a cashmere sweater from the new friend she just can't shake off. In the Rovers Return, Alma tells Mike and Audrey she wants to fix Hayley up with a fella, but Mike wonders who would have Hayley, saying she's nothing but a geek. Alma wonders who would be desperate enough to go out with Hayley–and just at that moment, into the Rovers walks Curly. All eyes turn toward him. 'What?' he says, looking around at them all.

Alma invites Curly for dinner at her flat. She invites Hayley and Audrey as support, then Roy as a spare bloke to make up the numbers. Mike decides he's not staying in for dinner with the 'trainspotting society' and promptly leaves. Audrey gets hideously drunk, and when Curly tells Alma he wants to leave after dinner, Audrey blurts out that the only reason he was invited was for him to get together with Hayley. Everyone is embarrassed and hugely upset, except Audrey, who is having a whale of a time.

Roy decides to leave too and offers to share a taxi with Hayley–but the two cheeky monkeys don't go straight home; they head off to the Rovers for a chat about how patronising some people can be.

There's a twinkle in Roy's eye when Hayley tells him that night, 'I want to lead my own life and live it my way,' but he doesn't yet fully know what she means. And when he finds out, there'll be tears– just you wait and see.

Hayley and Roy's friendship develops as they recognise in each other the loneliness they both feel that comes from being an outsider, from being different to the rest of the world. When Hayley walks into the café to hear Gail yelling at Roy, 'It's true what everyone around here says. You are mentally retarded!' she sees Roy's shocked face and asks him if he's okay. With one word that breaks Hayley's heart, Roy quivers a bit and replies 'No.'

Gail has the decency to apologise to Roy later and hug him. Roy, obviously never having hugged anyone before, is unsure how to handle this and tells Gail she'd better let go of him in case anyone should walk into the café and get the wrong idea.

As their friendship grows, Roy takes Hayley out to dinner and helps her take off her red anorak as they take their table. They both admit they've never been on a proper date with anyone else before and raise their glasses to Alma, with much gratitude, for bringing them together.

Romance, stain remover and bus timetables

Hayley even helps out at the Red Rec with Roy,
taking along a box of lemon meringues from
Firman's. Spider has been digging tunnels at the Red
Rec in his eco–quest to save the hoary ground wort,
and the meringues go flying as Roy and Hayley fall
down into one of the holes. Hayley hurts her leg and
Roy rubs it better.
'How does that feel?' asks Roy.
'Lovely!' she replies.
He takes Hayley to the Rovers for a drink afterwards
and presents her with a gift–stain remover–to take the
mud off her anorak. It's the start of something special,
we can tell, and it develops slowly and beautifully.

Roy invites Hayley for Sunday lunch, but Hayley's
bus is delayed, so they eat in Jim's café instead,
discussing bus timetables, life, the universe and
everything. Roy has something he desperately wants
to ask Hayley but each time he plucks up the courage
he's interrupted by Fred, and then Curly, who come
into the café wanting something to eat, assuming the
place is still open. Roy tells Hayley he feels they have
so much in common after Hayley confesses she liked
woodworking and technical drawing at school more
than she enjoyed domestic science.

Hayley tells Roy her big secret

When Roy and Hayley get cosy in the café after Roy
cooks them a romantic meal one night, he asks her if
she'd like to take coffee in his flat. Hayley tells Roy
there is something he should know first. This is the
moment when Hayley decides to trust Roy with her

greatest secret.

'What is it?' Roy asks.

'It is something to do with my past ...' Hayley begins.

'Your past?' Roy says, a little confused.

'Several years past, now,' she says, before coming straight out with it. 'I'm a transsexual. I mean, I'm a female not by birth, but by choice.'

Poor Roy, the news hits him hard. He tells Hayley he understands things like stamps, aircraft and trains. He likes to put things in columns, but this ... this he just doesn't know how to deal with. He asks her to leave, and she does. Later, Hayley tries to talk to Roy in the Rovers, but he is too confused and walks away from her, muttering, 'Leave me alone.'

Hayley decides to confide to Alma that she is a transsexual. She is relieved when Alma is hugely supportive of her as a friend. Alma then speaks to Roy and tells him that she knows the truth about Hayley. She advises a hurt and confused Roy to write down his feelings for Hayley, and to let Hayley know how much he values her friendship. This he does, and in a truly touching scene, he reads out his letter to Hayley in the middle of a crowded street.

'Dear Hayley ...' he begins. The letter goes on to describe how Roy is touched by Hayley's friendship and how much he wants to remain friends with her. Roy finishes reading the letter with the words: 'Yours faithfully, Roy Cropper.'

The operation

Roy and Hayley make up as friends and meet later for a fruit juice in the Rovers. They chat along quite nicely until Hayley announces she has received a letter from the hospital about her operation. *The* operation. There is silence. Then she tells Roy that she hopes they can still be friends afterwards. Roy confirms that they will.

A few days later, Hayley comes into Jim's café and tells Roy that she has been to see her solicitor. It looks like she is going to come into some money, a lot of money, as she was the only beneficiary of her late father's will. This means she can afford to go abroad and have her operation done privately and discreetly in Amsterdam.

Roy, prepared for Hayley's departure, gives her a gift. It is a book on automotive engines, but when Hayley opens the book there is a silver locket inside, a token of his affection for her.

As Hayley prepares to leave for her operation abroad, they say their goodbyes. Roy offers his hand for Hayley to shake, but instead she grabs him in a bear hug and thanks him for everything he has done. 'You made me feel like a real woman,' she tells him. Shyly, Roy asks if Hayley has found him attractive. 'Oh yes,' she replies. 'Attractive and interesting.' They tell each other to take care, and as Hayley leaves for Amsterdam, Roy gives the thumbs up sign.

After her operation in Amsterdam, Hayley takes time out to recuperate and writes Roy a letter. It is a letter which brings Roy all the way from Weatherfield to Holland to find Hayley. After spending a few days together, unsuccessfully trying to find out how they feel about each other, Hayley finally receives a sign from Roy that he really cares a great deal. When he leaves for the airport to head home, Roy leaves behind an engraved watch as a present for Hayley. As a result, Hayley dashes to the airport and catches up with Roy. Through the security window of the departure lounge, Hayley catches Roy's eye and writes on the glass with her red lip pencil.

'I'm coming with you!' Roy is overjoyed, and tears of happiness roll down Hayley's face.

First kiss

Back in Weatherfield, Roy and Hayley decide to start their relationship again and try once more. But with neither of them having any experience, they're not really sure how to begin. They talk things through on a seat by the boating lake.

'Where do we start?' wonders Roy.

'I expect we'll have to play it by ear,' Hayley replies.

'Perhaps if I kissed you?' he offers.

'I don't mind,' Hayley says as she turns her face to Roy, and the two of them share their very first kiss.

As the two of them grow closer, one night they sort through Hayley's dad's belongings. Roy comes across a photograph album which has spaces on most pages where pictures have been removed. Hayley tells Roy her father took the photos out and threw them in the fire on the day she told him she wanted to be a woman. In the back of a drawer, Roy finds a photo of Hayley as a child. There is an awkwardness between them, but later in the Rovers, Roy presents Hayley with the photo which he has had framed. He tells her, 'Don't bury the past. It has made you what you are today.'

One of the factory girls

In need of work, Hayley approaches Mike Baldwin at the factory and asks him for a job as a machinist. Mike turns her down flat without any explanation. He has never liked Hayley. Later, in the Rovers, Roy places a bet with Mike that if Hayley doesn't prove she is the fastest machinist he has ever seen then he will pay Mike £50. Mike considers this, raises the bet to £100 and says if Hayley does prove to be the best, he will give her a job. Needless to say, she gets the job, with Mike telling Alma:
'She can sew like an angel ... worth two of Ida Clough!'

When Hayley starts work at the factory she is a little nervous about meeting the other girls there, so she takes in a bag of humbugs to share on her first day. Roy gives Hayley some advice on her first day at work.
'Best keep well to yourself,' he says, worried about the lager lout, uncouth mentality of the workforce.
'I think I know more about how to be one of the girls than you do,' she replies, smiling.

Hayley is so quick and efficient at her work that she has the other girls wondering what she is up to. Ida Clough is loudest in voicing her mistrust of Hayley, wondering if she is really a spy for Baldwin. Hayley soon wins the girls over after offering to do their work for them, and feels she is getting on fine, fielding questions from them about Roy. When one of the girls tells her that she thinks Roy is a bit weird, Hayley defends him immediately with force and passion.
'Roy is lovely!' she says.

Hayley receives her first wage packet from Baldwin but is still paying tax on the emergency code. Mike tells her it is because of a computer error, that the tax office records show her as 'Harry'. Mike brushes the mistake off and says he is sure it will get sorted out soon. He goes home to Alma, joking about the tax office mistakenly calling Hayley by the wrong name of Harry. Alma assumes that Mike knows that Hayley actually was called Harry, so she tells Mike all about Hayley's past. Mike doesn't quite know what to say and eventually comes out with a shocked: 'Flippin' Ada!'

Now that he knows about Hayley, it hardens Mike's attitude towards her even further, and he tells Alma he is going to sack her. Alma invites Hayley to the flat for lunch and confesses that she has told Mike. Hayley is worried that Mike will tell the others, but Alma gives her assurance it won't go any further. Hayley then confides in Roy about what has happened and is worried her secret might be made public. Roy is worried too, but for whom– his own sake or Hayley's?

Hayley returns to the factory and determines to tell the girls the truth about why she was sacked. Both Mike and Alma advise her to keep quiet, with Mike warning her. 'These aren't *Guardian* readers, you know. They are going to think you're a weirdo, just a bloke in a frock.' In the Rovers, Hayley plucks up the courage and decides to tell Janice and Ida the truth. Just as she is about to tell them, loudmouth Audrey bursts in on their conversation. This makes Hayley realise that these backstreet Weatherfield women can't possibly understand what she has been through, and she decides to keep quiet for now.

With her new job settled, Hayley decides to start looking for a new place to live. She wants to live closer to the factory–and to Roy. Roy suggests she has a look at the new flats that Steve McDonald is building and tells her he will accompany her to the viewing at the weekend.

Roy proposes to Hayley

With a bit of encouragement from Gail, Roy finally picks up the courage to ask Hayley to move into his flat with him. 'You'll be no inconvenience,' he tells her. So, with her bags packed, Hayley arrives at the café, and they head upstairs together. Hayley, resplendent in new frilly nightie is expecting to share the only bed in the flat with Roy. Roy, however, has other plans and sleeps on the fold–out bed in the living room. He tells Hayley he believes they should marry first before taking the relationship any further, and on bended knee, he proposes. Hayley knows that she has no choice but to turn him down.
'We can't ever get married Roy, not until there's a change in the law. '
'Oh, I see, ' says Roy, although it is clear he doesn't see, not really. 'Do you think we ought to wait for that, then? The change in the law?'
'I think we'll have a pretty long wait. It is not on, Roy, marriage. It is just not one of our options.'

The next night, Roy dims the lights, cooks a meal in the flat and opens a bottle of wine. On the stereo in the background, the strains of 'The Lady in Red' and '(You Make Me Feel Like) A Natural Woman' can be heard as Roy admits he doesn't have much experience in the ways of 'you know'; in fact, he doesn't have any experience at all. He confesses that he has been to the library to look for a book on the subject of, 'you know'. Hayley, relieved, tells Roy that she also doesn't have any experience of, 'you know'.

Roy pipes up, 'Well, if neither of us know what we're doing, then we won't know if we're doing it wrong, will we?'

And with that, he leads Hayley by the hand to the bedroom. They spend the night together, in the same room and in the same bed. The next morning at breakfast they discuss everything about the previous night–curtains, duvets, sunlight streaming in through the window–everything except what they really feel about one another.

Trouble at the factory

When Roy suggests they go away for a long weekend, Hayley says she'll ask Mr. Baldwin for time off at work. Later in the Rovers, Mike lays into Roy about his weekend away with Hayley.

'I hear you and your friend are going on holiday soon,' Mike says. 'Where are you going? Thailand?'

'Wh … why do you say that?' wonders Roy.

'Well, I thought you and your partner would go somewhere exotic.'

'I'm not with you,' Roy says.

Mike pushes things further. 'Well, it'd be just up your street there. I mean, anything goes, gender–wise. '

Roy's confused but starting to get angry. 'I beg your pardon?'

'Weirdos. Freaks.' Mike laughs.

'I resent that.'

'If she's not a freak,' says Mike, nodding towards
Hayley, 'I'm the Queen Mother. All right?'
Roy quietly suggests that Mike step outside, and when
he refuses, mild–mannered Roy is pushed to extremes
and throws a pint of beer in Baldwin's face.

Back at work, Hayley goes to see Mike in his office,
to beg him, please, not to cause a fuss. She tells him
that all she wants to do is live a normal life. But when
Mike makes remarks about her 'having her wedding
tackle cut off', Hayley know he is going to remain
bigoted and that nothing will change his attitude.
Mike spends much of his time deliberately picking on
Hayley, and the other girls just can't figure out why he
is being so nasty to her.

In the Rovers later Mike greets Roy and Hayley at the
bar with:
'Evening, lads!' and bellows out 'Patterson!' to
Hayley across the factory floor.
Hayley, certain that Mike is going to tell the girls
what he knows about her, steels herself to tell them
herself. Roy is against her plan. He wants her to keep
quiet but Hayley, determined as always, comes right
out with it and tells the girls in the factory that she is a
transsexual.

Only Liz McDonald shows any concern for Hayley's
true feelings. The others, including Janice, make
jokes. Linda refuses to let Hayley use the ladies' toilet
at work, calling her 'a pervert'. Baldwin tells Hayley
to use the gents' loo, but Hayley refuses, and quite
rightly so.

Word spreads, and soon everyone knows about Hayley's past. Only Alma and Liz are supportive, along with Gail, who tells Hayley:
'You'll always be my favourite couple. Come round to us any time for supper.'
Toyah wants to be supportive to Roy and Hayley but seems a bit confused by the whole thing. Les proves true to type–being downright ignorant and rude, and unfortunately telling all and sundry exactly what he feels about Hayley being 'A fella in a dress with his tackle chopped off.'

Sleeping partners

Roy and Hayley's relationship continues and deepens, despite the hostility directed towards them from Baldwin, Les and some of the others they once thought of as friends. Meanwhile at Jim's café, Gail tells Roy she has decided to sell her share of the business. When Hayley tells Roy she wants to be supportive of him in his new venture, he takes this to mean she wants to be his business partner. Roy tells Gail he'll not be needing her any more anyway, as Hayley is going to help out in the new place. However, this is not what Hayley meant at all. To clear up the confusion, Hayley asks Gail if she'll stay on at the new place and tells Roy she'll invest in the café as a sleeping partner.

1999

Frothy Coffee

Roy has big plans for his new café on Coronation Street and renames it Roy's Rolls. He invests in a second–hand espresso machine, but it won't work properly, and as the instructions are in Italian, he can't understand how it works. Hayley comes to his rescue by translating some of the key words, but soon realises the instructions are for a washing machine, not a coffee maker. Roy has doubts about moving his business to the new café, but Hayley has every faith in her Roy–that is, until Hayley spots Roy nipping out of the flat on an evening and lying to her about where he is going. She confides in Linda and Janice at the factory and both of them, basing events on blokes they have known and loved, decide Roy is having an affair.
'If your bloke's cheating on you, you are one of the girls finally,' says Linda. 'Join the club.'

Hayley decides to follow Roy to see what he gets up to at night when he slips out of the flat. With Linda and Janice in tow, Hayley follows Roy to a secret address, where a woman welcomes him indoors and takes his anorak off. Egged on by Linda and Janice, Hayley confronts Roy when he arrives home. She asks him what he has been up to and where he has been going. Roy tells her the truth–that he has been having dancing lessons in preparation for the Valentine disco. However, when Hayley tells Linda and Janice this news, they think Hayley has been duped and that Roy is lying to cover the fact he is really having an affair.

Hayley decides to follow Roy again when he goes for his next dancing lesson. As Hayley is snooping around outside the house, Roy looks out of the window and spies Hayley, and in her surprise at being spotted she falls into the flowerbed. Roy is bitterly disappointed in Hayley for her lack of trust in him and tells her quite sternly:

'This is no basis for a long-term relationship!'

As the date of the Valentine disco draws near, Hayley helps Alison to prepare the decorations for the night.

'I think you're really brave,' says Alison

To which Hayley replies:

'I'm nothing much without Roy.'

Proposal at the disco

At the Valentine disco, Roy is wearing a *Saturday Night Fever* white suit complete with medallion. He sits down next to Hayley and proposes to her with his grandmother's ring.

'I love you, Hayley,' he says, 'and I want to marry you. Now, I know that will be difficult, but I'm very determined. However. Wherever. We'll find a way. But in the meantime, I want you to wear this ring so everybody will know my commitment to you and, well, hopefully your commitment to me.'

Hayley accepts, and Roy slips the antique ring onto Hayley's finger.

Wedding No. 1, April 1999

Roy receives his very first lesson on the Internet, from Curly, when he decides to look for a church that will recognise an alternative blessing. They meet Jessica, a new vicar at Emily's church, who agrees to marry them.

Roy wants a small do, about ten guests, but Hayley wants all her friends to be there. Hayley and Roy plan their wedding, with Hayley asking Alma to be matron of honour, and Toyah's chuffed to be asked to be bridesmaid. Roy is less sure who to ask to be his best man, and Hayley has to deter him from asking Gail, so he asks Martin instead. They plan their honeymoon in York, and Hayley starts making her wedding dress using a sewing machine in the factory.

On the day of Roy and Hayley's wedding, Hayley is in her dressing gown at Alma's when Audrey and Maxine arrive to do her hair and make-up. Over at Roy's flat, best man Martin calms a nervous Roy. Hayley's Aunty Monica and Uncle Bert arrive at Alma's flat, and Hayley tells them both how happy she is that they have turned up, to which (her not very understanding) Uncle Bert replies:
'Come on now Harold, put a pair of trousers on and come home with me and your Aunty.'

Les wonders what Toyah is doing all dressed up, and when she tells him she is going to be bridesmaid for Roy and Hayley, he bans her from attending and sends her up to her room. Assisted by Spider, Toyah escapes through her bedroom window and heads to the wedding. Everyone is on their way to the church, but what they do not know yet is that Les has tipped off the press about the unusual nuptials about to take place. As the wedding party makes its way to the church, there are press and photographers waiting for them all to arrive.

It is Emily who finds out what Les has gone and done.
She manages to stop Roy and Martin's wedding car
before they get to the church.
'I don't want that lot mobbing her,' Roy tells Martin,
worried about the journalists' reactions to Hayley.
Roy then manages to stop Hayley's wedding car, and
breaks the devastating news to Hayley that their
wedding is off... or is it?

Mr. and Mrs Cropper

Everyone in the wedding party traipses back to the
café, disappointed by the events of the day and angry
with Les. Roy and Hayley have a heart to heart, and
she thanks him for trying to make her dream day
come true. However, all is not lost. With all the guests
in the café and the bride and groom there too, Jessica
holds a ceremony right there and then and blesses the
relationship, with (the slightly more understanding
this time) Uncle Bert giving the bride away. Just when
Roy thinks he couldn't be any happier, Hayley
surprises him by announcing she has had her surname
changed by deed poll from Patterson to Cropper.

As the happy couple leave Weatherfield for their
honeymoon in York, Hayley throws the bouquet into
the small crowd of guests. It is hard to know who is
more surprised, Ken or Deirdre, when Deirdre catches
it squarely. Janice takes one of the pans tied to the
back of the wedding car and chases Les down the
cobbles with it for spoiling Roy and Hayley's church
blessing.

After Roy and Hayley return from honeymoon, there is a lot of love in Roy's Rolls. When Gail asks Roy how the baked beans are coming on, he quotes Shakespeare in reply. He says he couldn't be happier that since the wedding he and Hayley have become even more accepted on the Street.

Flirting and fighting

At Roy's Rolls, Hayley gets an admirer when Stuart, one of the builders on the Victoria Court development, starts flirting and chatting her up. Hayley gets all flirty and flighty, but Roy doesn't notice what is going on–until Les Battersby blabs to Stuart about Hayley's past. There is a fight in the café when Stuart, ego dented, has a go at Roy, who is saved from having to fight back by Jim McDonald's timely intervention.

Meanwhile at the factory, Hayley's having a hard time as Gwen takes time off for shopping when she ought to be working. Hayley confides in Roy that she is not really cut out for this supervisory business.
'I see myself more as the captain of the rounders team than Attila the Hun.'

A child for the Croppers

Roy waxes lyrical one day about an allotment where he'd like to grow organic vegetables for use in the café. Hayley wonders aloud who they'll hand the café to once they are gone, family–wise. Neither of them looks comfortable discussing such things and Hayley looks away, sipping on her orange juice. But now the issue has been raised, Roy admits to Hayley he is not ready to have a child. But he can see how much Hayley wants to be a mother, and finally agrees to go through the adoption process. They send off for the forms to complete and Roy fills in the form with his fountain pen, to lend an air of respectability to the matter. Inside, he is worried for Hayley, not yet knowing how the law stands in respect to their search for a child.

They get a visit from a man, a very nice man, from the adoption agency, and Roy slowly and gently warms to the idea of becoming a dad, for Hayley's sake more than his own. He wonders what they'll do when the baby arrives. 'It'll need full–time surveillance,' he muses, before setting off to make a checklist of things they need to do before a child arrives.

The Croppers are honest right from the start with the man from the adoption agency. When he hears Hayley's news, he says:
'There's nothing in the rules that say you have to be a conventional couple.'
Discussing things later, Hayley wonders what sort of child they will get, saying to Roy:
'We might get one like you.'
'No,' says Roy. 'No, I wouldn't wish that on anyone.'

Foster-child Wayne Hayes

Roy and Hayley's first foray into foster care is with a child called Wayne Hayes, a small kid wearing glasses and with ginger hair. Wayne's stepdad Alex pays Roy and Hayley a visit, saying that Wayne needs £60 for a new pair of trainers. Roy, soft touch that he is, hands the money over. The Croppers then find out that Wayne has been given another foster home. It unsettles them a bit, as they would have dearly loved to have fostered him themselves. They talk things through with the very nice man from the agency, then Wayne's dad returns, telling Roy how much he'd have liked Wayne to have been fostered by the Croppers instead of the family that Wayne is now with. He then goes on to say Wayne wants to go on a school trip, but they can't afford to send him, and could Roy give him the cash? It is too much for Roy, who finally loses his temper and chases Alex out of the café. Roy knows he might be a soft touch, but he is also no fool.

The Croppers are then called to a meeting with the council and are over the moon to find out they have been approved as suitable foster parents. Hayley wants to get started on decorating the spare room, while Roy is more cautious and admits he feels somewhat scared. 'I'm just not used to being accepted.'

Foster-child Jackie

The Croppers are then given a 15-year-old girl called Jackie, whose mum has had to go into hospital, and she has no one else to care for her. In preparation for Jackie's arrival, Hayley pops into The Kabin to buy teen magazines. She wants to find out what is in the minds of 15-year-old girls, as it is a subject she knows nothing about.

Hayley goes overboard with kindness to Jackie. She offers her food, drink and hospitality till she is blue in the face. But all Jackie wants to do is get out of the flat and be with her friends. Finally, Roy, Hayley and Jackie go bowling together. Armed with his little instruction book and dressed in jeans (Jeans! Roy!), Roy gets the hang of it and even manages a strike. But he is less happy that Jackie is making friends with the Grimshaw boys, Sarah Lou and Candice as the gang gather round the bus stop for snogging and chips. 'But what if she gets pregnant?' Roy worries.

The Croppers learn the rules of parenting slowly, but very, very surely. They worry themselves sick over Jackie being broken–hearted when they thought she fancied Jason Grimshaw only to find out that Jason had his eye on someone else. What else can Roy do but console Jackie with macaroni cheese and sticky toffee pudding in the café? Prepared for a crying match and a teenage tantrum when Jackie returns to the flat, Roy and Hayley are somewhat surprised when she is as happy as Larry after being asked out by another boy at school.

Foster-child Fiz Brown

On Roy and Hayley's second wedding anniversary, Roy wants to spend time with his wife at the boating lake where they shared their first kiss. But his plans are thrown awry by the arrival of their second foster-child, a girl called Fiona–or Fiz, for short. Fiz is somewhat lively and soon has Hayley out shopping for clothes that Roy doesn't approve of. Worse is to come when Fiz sets the café on fire when the Croppers are out at the Rovers. There is smoke and flames everywhere, but when Roy chastises Fiz for the mess she has caused, Hayley chastises Roy for the way he is berating poor Fiz.

They receive a visit from Mr. Hartnell from the council, who tells them that Fiz has complained about Roy being violent towards her. Poor Roy, the only thing he would ever batter are pancakes, the only things he would ever whip are eggs, the only time he would give a good roasting is to a chicken dinner. Mr. Hartnell is duty-bound to remove Fiz from their care and investigate further. Sarah-Lou comes to the rescue when she tells Hayley that Fiz had said she'd been planning to get Roy into trouble because she did not like him. Everything gets settled in the end, but not until Roy is beset by doubts about fostering ever again.

Wayne again

Roy then pays five thousand pounds to Alex Swinton in exchange for his stepson, Wayne Hayes, who returns to the Croppers' lives. When Hayley finds out what Roy has done, she is furious, but secretly happy to have a child of their own at last. Wayne's mum Sheila comes round in a strop, bringing back the money.
'He's my son, my Wayne, and he is not for sale.'
But she soon realises that Wayne will have a better

life without getting beaten up by Alex on a regular basis. She takes the cash back and leaves Wayne with Roy and Hayley. As the Croppers adjust to life in their tiny flat with an extra person around, Wayne doesn't settle well and starts wetting the bed. Terrified that Hayley will be mad with him, he doesn't mention it to her. But Roy and Hayley offer nothing to Wayne except their total affection, support and loving concern.

As the Croppers play happy families, Wayne's stepdad Alex finds out the truth about Hayley's past and threatens Roy that he is going to tell Wayne. Panicked, Roy decides, with half an hour to spare, that he is taking Hayley and Wayne on a camping trip. 'Let's be impetuous for once!' he tells Hayley. 'We are masters of our destiny.'
He is clearly a worried man, scared of losing Wayne, and so off they go camping with Martin and Sally.

At the campsite in the woods, Alex has followed the Croppers to the countryside and grabs poor Wayne. Wayne screams and Roy and Hayley go running to his aid. There is a bit of argy–bargy and Alex storms off to call Social Services to tell them the Croppers have kidnapped Wayne.

There is nothing else for Roy and Hayley to do but be honest and tell Wayne what is going on. They had already told Wayne the truth about Hayley and were surprised when he took it so well. Wayne compared Hayley's gender realignment to that of earthworms and tropical fish. It prompted Roy to comment to Hayley, 'I'm just glad he sees you as part of the wonder and diversity of nature'.

They give Wayne the option of going back to Weatherfield and all the trouble that will bring or leaving with the Croppers for somewhere new. Wayne decides he wants to stay with Roy and Hayley, and while the others are in the campsite shop, the three of them speed away in Martin's car. 'I haven't driven in years!' cries Hayley as she leans over to Roy in a panic. 'And I don't know what to do!'

"Kid Disappears in Tranny Snatch"

So screams the front-page headline of *The Weatherfield Gazette*. As Roy and Hayley hide out with Wayne in the country, Wayne writes an open letter to the papers, telling the press he is happy to be with the Croppers. Wayne's letter states that he has come to no harm, but it does little good. Roy is getting desperate; he wants to escape to Ireland and has not shaved for a fortnight. Hayley tries to make him see sense and finally the Croppers do the right thing and turn themselves in to the police.

But it is too late!

Roy and Hayley have already been spotted and reported to the authorities. They are arrested on the charge of abduction, kept in the cells overnight then questioned the next day. Roy is in a real state, desperate to get the truth out about Wayne's evil stepdad Alex, who beats up his son, but the police can only go by the report from Social Services, which proves nothing and does little to help Roy and Hayley.

Meanwhile, Wayne moves back in with his mum and Alex at home, who has threatened Wayne already to keep his mouth shut about being beaten up. An ineffectual social worker calls round to see Wayne, and in the presence of Alex, Wayne has no choice but to say things are fine.

At the magistrate's court, the locals are out in force to cheer on the Croppers. Blanche takes along a bag of pear drops to suck as she settles in for the court case. Because of the seriousness of the charge of abduction, the judge has no choice but to refer the case to Crown Court. He grants bail to Roy and Hayley on condition they do not leave the country or contact Wayne. Roy seems happy to accept these conditions but Hayley less so. She lets the judge know, in no uncertain terms, that she is not at all happy, and she is remanded in custody.

Arrested and in prison

In prison, Hayley has a hard time. Persecuted by the other prisoners and beleaguered by a butch bully, she is not enjoying life in the big house at all. She puts on a brave face when Roy visits, but he soon discovers the others know Hayley's past and are giving her grief. They know that she is a transsexual and even that her old name was Harold. Disheveled and depressed, Roy goes to Wayne's house and pleads with Wayne's mum Sheila to tell the truth, but she is too scared of Alex to speak out.

Back on the Street, Roy's flat is in a mess and Fiz helps him clean up. Roy gets a shock visit from Sheila with Wayne in tow. Sheila has been beaten black and blue by Alex and wants Roy to take her to the police station, as she is ready to tell the truth about Alex once and for all. As the three of them go off to the station, Alex comes into the café looking for Roy. Vera does a good job of stalling him to give the others time to get to the police station before he catches them up. At the police station, just as Sheila is ready to make her statement, Alex bursts in and it takes two policemen and Roy to restrain him from beating her up anymore. Once Sheila's made her statement, Roy sets things in motion to have Hayley freed and although she is happy to be home, she is soon cornered by journalists wanting her side of the story.

2002

History repeats itself

Roy is elected for the position of Chair of the
Weatherfield Historical Society. Hayley is very
pleased for him, even if he was the only candidate.
Roy is in his element, organising a historical event to
coincide with the Queen's Golden Jubilee
celebrations. He obtains permission from the
Historical Society to organise an event, and pores
over old maps of the Red Rec until he finds out that a
famous battle was fought there.
'Why is it called red?' he asks Hayley, who replies
that it is because of the red asphalt. Clearly getting
into his stride, Roy ponders aloud:
'Ah! But perhaps it was the red of the blood that was
spilt in 1642!'

Roy rallies support for his roundheads and cavaliers
shindig, as Fred has renamed the historical re–
enactment of the battle of the Red Rec. But while
Fred may joke about it, Roy takes it very seriously. At
a meeting in the café, Fred wants to liven up the event
with pies and ales and the good name of Elliott as the
number one sponsor, but Roy is less keen. Fred says
he wants a beer tent added to the agenda, while Norris
wants to discuss chemical toilets.

As Roy ploughs on with the plans for the historic
battle re–enactment, Fred edges his way in, and it
becomes more of a Roy versus Fred battle event. Fred
wants things done his way, injecting more humour
and action into the event, while Roy wants it done
properly, historically and authentically. And Norris?

He turns from Roy's camp to Fred's with the lure of a fancy costume, a pie and free ale from Fred.

'If you can't fight, wear a big hat. It is a saying round our way,' Norris says.

Roy is clearly disappointed that no one wants to take the event as seriously as he does, although Hayley does her best to cheer him on.

When Fred and Roy rally their troops to do battle on the Red Rec, there is a clash of egos and the realisation by Roy that this time, perhaps, his obsessive behaviour has got a bit out of line. Roy decides he needs a musket and hires one from a fellow reader of *Civil War Journal.* Deciding to unsheathe it in Freshco to do a test drill, Roy gets arrested and kept overnight in the cells on charges of endangering public safety and using threatening behaviour. 'But I only came in for shoe polish,' he says.

Roy gets grilled at the police station then released just in time to do battle on the Red Rec. There is a Rovers beer tent, an ice cream van, a tug–o–war team and the Bessie Street twirling kazoo band. Archie is the compère, and when the battle commences both teams stick to their scripts, for a while at least, and the skirmish begins. As rehearsed, Curly kills Les. Emma kills Kirk and Roy looks bemused. Norris kills Emma (with a certain amount of drama, passion and style) and Fred kills Ken. And then, oh then, it is time for Fred to kill Roy, but Roy's got other plans.

Fred's team has played dirty, deviating from the agreed plan and bringing shame to the skirmish with a pantomime horse and free pies. And Roy has had enough–he refuses to die! The two of them argue and trade personal insults. 'I'd rather be a showman than an anorak!' says Fred. Ouch. Then Roy makes a remark about Fred's wives always leaving him. Double ouch. Finally, somehow, the battlefield turns into a real fight, with pies being thrown and egos being dented. But it doesn't end there, oh no.

Back on the cobbles, the two teams separate. One team repairs to the café and the other to the Rovers to decide their next steps. Roy comes out of the café. Fred comes out of the Rovers. Think John Wayne, you get the idea. The camera does a close-up of Fred's face then Roy's face, then an even closer shot of Fred's eyes then Roy's eyes. This is serious stuff. Both have been humiliated and neither will admit defeat or apologise. Roy takes a pike, Fred stumbles and falls, and Roy raises the pike above Fred in his finery, lying there on the ground. There is a manic look on Roy's face; has he finally flipped? Will he plunge the pike? Of course not, but seeing Roy overtaken by his obsession was somewhat disturbing.

Fred and Roy finally shake hands and make up after Roy admits:
'I behaved in a petty and infantile manner.'
Roy tries to explain to Hayley how his raging emotions and violent feelings came to the fore as he cornered Fred on the cobbles. Nervous Hayley is not listening to him too much, not as he is fondling a huge knife in the café as he speaks.

Hayley's upset later when Roy flies off to Paxos on the Weatherfield Historical Society trip to ancient Greece. With his hot flask and his sandwiches for the plane journey, Roy heads to the airport in a taxi.

Hayley sheds a tear and wonders how she'll get through Christmas without him.

2003

Poor Roy. He doesn't like change. He likes things just the way they are, thank you very much. And then young whippersnapper Ciaran comes in with his plans for extending the café, forcing Roy to think well outside of his comfort zone. Ciaran's plans make Roy ruminate, cogitate, contemplate and agitate. But when Ciaran refers to Roy's Rolls as nothing more than 'a backstreet naff caff,' it is the ultimate insult, and more than Roy deserves. He tells Ciaran any deal he may have been considering is now well and truly off, but Ciaran has got plans of his own. After talking to Spider about his organic juice–bar, Ciaran tells Roy if he won't join him, he'll beat him. He plans to open up next door to Roy, selling fancy frothy coffee, contemporary cappuccino and lah–di–dah latte.

Roy's all of a flutter:
'I feel like I've harboured a viper in my bosom,' he tells Hayley.
He then demands that Ciaran takes off his pinny–and promptly sacks him on the spot.

Toxic Tracy and the baby bet

Roy is in a dilemma. He thinks he has a secret admirer after Bev chatted him up, but Bev was just doing it for a laugh with the girls in the Rovers. Roy seeks counsel from men in the know about such matters– Fred and Harry. Harry gives him a copy of *Men are from Mars, Women are from Venus,* but Roy needs some proper advice on how to handle the situation. Meanwhile, Hayley finds out about the flirting joke Bev played on Roy and gives her a ticking off for being cruel to Roy. Roy tells Hayley that Harry has advised him to confront Bev in case her crush on him festers. Hayley relieves Roy by breaking it to him gently but firmly that Bev was only having a laugh.

Tracy picks up on all of this and thinks how much fun she could have by flirting with Roy herself. She makes a one-penny bet with Bev that she can get Roy into bed. Tracy starts by flirting with Roy in the Rovers. He is put off reading his highway code as Tracy introduces a little mirror–signal–manoeuvre sequence of her own. She touches his arm and his leg and confuses him greatly. The next day she pretends to lose an earring on the cobbles, and when Roy finds it for her, she drags him into the Rovers to buy a drink for her hero. Too polite, too naive and too confused to understand what is happening, Roy finds himself beside Tracy in the bar just as Hayley comes in. Tracy makes it clear to Hayley she is flirting with Roy–as he tries to do his *Guardian* crossword. It is too much for Hayley and she lunges at Tracy with the ice bucket, shouting:
'Leave Roy alone!'
'I can have any man I want … well, not you, obviously,' Tracy yells back at Hayley.
Later in the Rovers, Hayley warns Roy to avoid eye contact with Tracy.
'Don't look at her, she's pouting!'

When Hayley's Uncle Bert is taken poorly and needs looking after, Hayley does her duty and goes to look after him. This leaves Roy alone with Tracy–and she is determined to get her claws into Roy. She spots her chance when she spies Roy alone at Peter and

Shelley's wedding reception and drops a date rape drug into his drink. It hits Roy hard. Roy is taken by Tracy back to the Barlows', up to her room and into her bed.

Roy is ashamed and thoroughly confused when he wakes the next morning beside Tracy. Lifting her discarded bra from one of his shoes on the floor, he gets dressed and tries to sneak out before Ken and Deirdre see him. Too late; he is spotted.
'Would you like a cup of tea, Roy?' asks Ken, confused to see Roy creeping out of his house.

Roy returns home and he showers, in tears, unaware of what has happened with Tracy. Back at the Barlows', Tracy confesses to Ken and Deirdre that it was all done for a bet and a bit of a laugh. Ken is disgusted and tells Tracy to pack her bags and get out. He calls round to see Roy to try to figure out what happened. The shame of it is too much for Roy; he is a destroyed man. He feels he has to take responsibility for his own actions and blames the glass of champagne that he drank at the wedding. Being unused to alcohol, he is blaming himself, little knowing that he was drugged by the strumpet of the Street for a one–penny bet and a very cruel joke.

After being thrown out of the house by Ken, Tracy goes to stay with Bev at the Rovers. Roy tries to remember what happened that night in Tracy's bed. He is unable to cope at first, so Ken helps Roy open up the café and Ken tells Roy about Tracy's one–penny bet.

Needless to say, gossip is rife about Roy spending the night with Tracy. In the Kabin, Norris puts two and two together to make a very unlikely four.
'Roy and Tracy?' he says, as his eyes twirl and his fingers twitch. 'Tracy and Roy?'

Roy goes to see Tracy at the Rovers for an explanation, but she takes responsibility for nothing and is not ashamed of what she did. Fiz visits Roy in the flat, and she finds a broken man. She gears up for a punch–up when she spies Tracy in the pub later. Giving her a good slap, Fiz tells Tracy:
'You mess with Roy again and I'll kill you!'

Bev wants Tracy out of the Rovers before Peter and Shelley return from honeymoon. With nowhere to live now, Emily takes Tracy in. Tracy confesses to Emily that she is pregnant and that as the baby must be Roy's, she is going to have an abortion.

Meanwhile Roy is beside himself with nerves as Hayley's return draws near. Jack advises Roy that honesty is never the best policy, and he should lie through his teeth to his missus. This is something that Roy never would or could do. When Hayley returns he is straight with her, in a roundabout way. He builds up the story, slowly and carefully, omitting no detail, and then comes straight out with the climax.
'I had relations with Tracy Barlow.'

Hayley is in shock at Roy's revelation. She has trouble believing that he cannot remember anything and asks if he could have been unconscious. Hayley decides to find out the truth by confronting Tracy herself. Tracy's now homeless, friendless, bitter and twisted and a nasty piece of work to boot. She decides to head back to London and hops into a taxi just as Deirdre spits out that she is ashamed she is her daughter. As the taxi pulls away from the cobbles, Hayley chases after it, demanding to know the truth from Tracy.

Roy is having a terrible time over what he thinks he did with Tracy, and he tells Hayley he is going to do the decent thing and move out. Hayley persuades him to stay, and the Croppers try to come to terms with the seismic change in their relationship.

When Tracy returns to the Street, Hayley marches round to the Barlows' with Roy at her heels, determined to find out the truth. But all Tracy can do is call Hayley names before she announces she is carrying the Cropper child.
'You're lying! And evil!' says Hayley.
'Pregnant?' says Roy.

Roy says he must do the right thing and provide for Tracy's baby. He asks Hayley if she can stand by him, but it is not something that Hayley can do. She packs to leave, assuming that what Roy has always wanted was a 'real' woman. Roy swears on little Bethany's life that he can't remember what happened in Tracy's bed that night. He continues to blame himself for what he says can only be described as his animal instincts.
'But you never get carried away!' says Hayley.
'Do you remember that cuddle on the sofa we had the other week,' replies Roy, 'when we were playing Scrabble, and I knocked the board away? We haven't seen the letter Q since.'

Hayley saves Roy from suicide

As Hayley packs to leave Roy asks if he can help. 'You can get my oestrogen,' Hayley says, before spending the night with Angela across the road. Meanwhile, at the flat, Roy starts knocking back the aspirin, one at a time, carefully and slowly. He leaves a note in the café with a 20p piece for whoever finds him to call the Samaritans. Fortunately, Hayley returns to the flat in the nick of time, finds Roy and gets him to hospital.

Hayley knows then that she can't, and won't, leave Roy. She decides to stand by him when he says he wants Tracy's baby to bring up as their own and when they put this to Tracy, she demands cash in exchange for the baby. She wants a lump sum, paid upfront, or she is going to the clinic for an abortion. Desperately pulling all their savings together and raiding the piggy bank, the Croppers hand Tracy all that they have and in the nick of time. It is just under £5,000, with the rest of the cash due when the baby is born. But after the money's handed over, Tracy flits to the Caribbean, leaving the Croppers even more angry, sad and confused.

Roy and Hayley reckon they have been more than patient with Tracy when she returns from holiday. They tell her they think the time's right for her to tell her parents she is pregnant. However, Tracy has plans of her own and shocks the Croppers when they find out she has started work as a Streetcars cab driver. Worse still, they find her drinking in the Rovers as she celebrates her divorce.

Finally, they corner Tracy in the Barlows' sitting room and the Croppers let Ken and Deirdre know about Tracy's baby. There is much screaming and yelling as Deirdre tells her daughter how disgusted she is with what she's done to poor Roy. Ken does an intake of breath when Deirdre shows how much she is ashamed of her daughter. 'That kidney was wasted on you.'

Tracy calls Roy 'a freak' and Deirdre calls Tracy 'a monster' and 'an evil little cow,' before the crying stops and the yelling ends. But Deirdre and Ken tell Tracy they will support her because she is carrying their grandchild which means they are somewhat surprised to hear Tracy say that she plans to give the baby to the Croppers when it is born. Of course, she omits to tell her parents that she is being paid for the baby.

Later at the Barlows', Ken wonders if Tracy's baby is really Roy's. When he shares his doubts with the Croppers, they storm round to see Tracy, who lies through her teeth and swears blind that the baby is Roy's.

Thinking he is the true father, there is only one way now for Roy to have legal claim on the baby–he has to marry Tracy. When Roy proposes to Tracy, she laughs in his face until Hayley gets stroppy. 'Marry Roy or the deal's off!'

At the dinner table in the Barlows', Tracy tells Peter everything–all about doping Roy, the baby's real father being Steve and the Croppers paying her cash for the child. Peter tells Tracy to come clean with Steve, see what his reaction is towards the baby being his and forget about the Croppers. And as all of this is going on, as Tracy tries to tell Steve the whole sordid truth at Streetcars, Roy and Hayley are with their bank manager, desperately trying to borrow more cash to give to Tracy.

Over at the factory, Hayley stuns the girls into silence when she announces she and Roy are having a baby. Fed up with two–faced Tracy, the Croppers are relieved that the news is finally out in the open about their bun in her oven. Tracy agrees to the plan to marry Roy and the pair of them sign up at Weatherfield register office to be wed.

When Deirdre's mum Blanche spots Tracy's baby bump, she demands to know who the dad is. When she finds out from Tracy that it is Roy, Blanche gives the Croppers a sharp and nasty piece of her mind and tells them the only way they'll get their hands on her great grandchild is over her dead body. She questions the Croppers' ability as parents with a final insult to Roy:
'... and you look as if you should be crayoning something!'

But there is a worse insult for the Croppers to come, worse than anything Blanche could spit at them. The lawyer who gave Roy the advice to marry Tracy so that he would have a legal claim over the baby mentions in passing that he doesn't have to do that. What he can do, instead, is sign a parental responsibility form which gives him the same rights. A further baby bombshell is dropped when

Tracy finally tells Steve he is the father of her baby and Steve tells Tracy he wants nothing to do with her.

2004

The birth of Patience Cropper / Amy Barlow

Roy and Hayley anticipate the arrival of Tracy's baby and decorate their spare room as a nursery. They even throw out their old jigsaws to make room in the flat. Roy frets endlessly about whether Tracy will sell or keep the baby when it is born. He picks up a cheap old–fashioned pram and Hayley points out how ridiculous it is, while Harry marvels at its solid British engineering. The Croppers even invest in a virtual baby–a crying, plastic doll that Roy insists will stand them in good stead to practise on before the real baby arrives. He even takes the virtual baby out for a walk, tucked into his shopping bag.

Tracy gives birth to a 6lb 4oz girl. Roy's allowed into the delivery room with Tracy under her strict instructions to 'stay at the top end'. Roy and Hayley are delighted with the baby, but the Barlows are livid and complain bitterly to Hayley that they're not being allowed into the delivery room when Roy is. It is all Hayley can do not to tell them about the money, but she lets slip that Tracy and Roy are married, which fairly quietens Blanche, for a minute at least. It shocks Ken and Deirdre, who can't understand why Tracy would have married Roy when there was nothing in it for her.

After the birth of the baby, Tracy gets straight on the phone to Steve to tell him about his daughter. Rushing to the phone, Tracy leaves the newly born baby crying in the room for Roy to find and comfort. Steve drives to the hospital and Tracy shocks him when she tells him about the cash deal with the Croppers. She says she will keep the baby if he leaves Karen and lives with her, but it is not something that Steve wants to do.

Back at the Barlows', Blanche and Deirdre are desperate for Tracy to keep her baby. The two women do all they can to massage whatever maternal instinct Tracy might have. It almost works, and Tracy starts to have doubts about giving the baby to the Croppers. When Roy and Hayley call round to collect the baby from her, she tells them she needs more time. Hayley screams the place down with anger and reminds Tracy that if she felt anything at all for the baby, she'd know she did not need time to think. As Roy and Hayley leave the house empty handed they hover on the doorstep, unsure what to do. Just then, Tracy comes out and hands them her baby and Roy hands her the final payment in exchange. As Tracy closes the door on her baby she breaks down in tears, but not before she has checked the Croppers' bank draft first.

Roy and Hayley are in their element, loving every single minute of being with their baby, whom they name Patience. Blanche is livid when she finds out what Tracy has done with the baby. She tells her granddaughter to move out of the house and, afraid of being homeless once more, it is only then that Tracy decides to get the baby back.

Showdown at Steve and Karen's wedding

Tracy Barlow certainly knows how to pick her moments. She arrives at Steve and Karen's wedding demanding to see Roy, who is there as a guest. Steve and Andy throw Tracy out, but she sneaks back into the church just as the bride and groom are at the altar. Tracy demands to see Roy, the wedding stops, accusing eyes turn toward her and everyone stands up to find out what is going on. Karen is livid and demands that Tracy leaves, but Tracy announces to everyone who the baby's real father is. It is not Roy's, she tells them, but Steve's.

Roy and Hayley sneak away with the baby as Steve and Karen repair to the vestry with Tracy. There are lies from Tracy, apologies to Karen from Steve and pure venom from Karen, who threatens Tracy with a spiked red stiletto heel. 'I've got one for each of you' she hisses at Steve when he tries to intervene. When Tracy leaves, Steve does his best to persuade Karen he still wants to marry her and he gets down on his knees and asks her all over again.

Back on the street, the Croppers know their time with baby Patience is limited. Sure enough, Tracy comes bawling at their door, demanding her baby back. Hayley stuns her into silence when she tells Deirdre, Ken and Blanche about the cash deal.

Despite everything, Ken and Deirdre tell Tracy they will support her, but Ken goes to see Roy for a chat. He knows the baby is better off with the Croppers but tells Roy that the law will see things differently. The Croppers are broken but have to do the right thing, and Roy returns baby Patience to Tracy before collapsing in tears outside the café. Knowing when they are beaten, the Croppers take to Whitby for a few days' rest.

'The sea can be very restorative,' muses Roy.

Tracy tries to change Patience's birth certificate, but it is harder than she thinks. To change the father's name from Roy to Steve, the registrar needs a DNA test from Steve–which he is not obliged to give. Tracy also wants to change the name Patience to Amy but officially has to do this by deed poll. It all proves a lot more bother than she expected it to be.

Meanwhile, the Croppers are crestfallen after a solicitor tells them they have no legal claim to baby Amy. That's when Roy comes up with a plan. He tells Tracy he wants their marriage annulled as soon as possible. He also tells her that in exchange for letting them look after Amy on occasion, he'll forego the monthly repayment on the money she owes them. Left without a babysitter, Tracy is straight round to the café asking the Croppers to look after Amy. It is a task which they do with much pleasure.

When Roy and Tracy's divorce finally comes through, the Croppers celebrate in the café with a candlelit dinner and Frankie Vaughan on the stereo. They take off on holiday soon after, with the spirit of adventure, a hot flask in their camper van, and a well-stocked hamper. They head off together to explore Britain's highways and byways with the help of an antique road atlas and a tartan picnic rug.

2005

Chesney Brown and the Venn diagram

Roy and Hayley are left to look after little Chesney, who is missing his mum Cilla when she goes on holiday to Spain. Roy helps Chesney with his maths homework in the café–it is Venn diagrams. He explains them to Chesney with the help of the salt cellar, a vinegar bottle and a packet of salt and vinegar crisps. Later, Roy and Hayley find Chesney on the Internet, trying to book a flight to Spain to see his mum using Roy's credit card. When Chesney says he feels he doesn't belong anywhere, that he is in a Venn diagram all of his own, Roy cuts out pictures of the Croppers and makes a special Venn diagram with Roy and Hayley on each side and Chesney in-between.

Contraption in the café

Roy receives news that his granddad has died. He frets about the family funeral, particularly meeting up with his dad, whom he never got on with. But his worries come to naught when Roy and Hayley are the only ones at the funeral to say their goodbyes.

Grandfather Cropper leaves a special gift for Roy in his will. It consists of plans for a machine designed to use energy expended by people coming into and going out of rooms. Roy's grandfather's plans, hopes and dreams of invention are passed on to Roy, who takes up the challenge of the contraption, starting right there in Roy's Rolls. Roy makes a Meccano model of his granddad's contraption before following the plans and making it for real. The café ceiling is covered in fans, pulleys, levers and switches.

'Eureka!' shouts Roy as Hayley wonders, exactly, just what it is that the contraption does.

Roy thinks the contraption is a testament to the genius of his grandfather. A hack from *The Gazette* turns up to look at the gizmo and to interview Roy.

'It is absolutely bonkers in a most amazing way,' he tells Roy.

Roy is sure the journalist will write a fitting story and indeed he does. News reaches Mr. Audenshaw from the Green Hotels chain who offers to buy Roy's grandfather's patent. Roy feels it impolite to refuse. The kinetic energy gizmo, says Mr. Audenshaw, will be installed on environmentally friendly hotel doors worldwide and will make Green Hotels rich. Roy's happy to sell the patent for the price of a new frame for his grandfather's photo.

Roy's Rolls fast becomes the talk of the north. The cooking in the café is credited in the national and local press. It is billed as 'the best full British breakfast in the whole of north–west England served without flourish or fanfare', just a dollop of brown sauce and plenty of salt. Further plaudits come Roy's way when he is crowned the unlikely darling of the bistro set. The sweet scent of success goes to Hayley's head and makes her giddy enough to suggest they open a bottle of sparkling wine to celebrate.

2006

Clifford turns up

Roy gets upset when he receives his school alumni newsletter, as it brings back painful school memories. The newsletter editor is a chap by the name of Clifford Ford, the one person at school who was even geekier than Roy. There is an article in the newsletter promoting a school reunion, and Roy decides to attend. But the trouble is, he is the only one who does turn up–apart from Clifford Ford. He is a strange bloke, this Clifford. He has an ASBO along with various injunctions and restraining orders against him from fellow schoolmates, and Roy is the only one who has spoken to him since 1975. Clifford is someone that even Roy feels uncomfortable being with, but he is too polite to say so. Clifford and the Croppers end up in the Rovers after the school reunion, and when Clifford goes home in a taxi Roy tells Hayley that he hopes Clifford doesn't get in touch with them ever again.

Unfortunately, he does.

Clifford pops into the café to see Roy and tells him he needs help doing up his model railway system. Roy's eyes light up! He chooses to spend time with his new old friend, much to Hayley's disdain.

'Hail Hayley!' Clifford says.
Then he presents her with a model railway figure dressed in a red anorak. She is not as happy to see Clifford as Roy is, who is becoming completely immersed in the model railway that Clifford's got

going. Roy and Clifford aim to rebuild the system and win a trophy for their efforts.

Hayley's not happy, though. Clifford gets his feet well under the table of life that is Roy and Hayley's marriage. Roy's in his element, choosing bits and pieces for the rail set, while Hayley can't ignore the fact that Roy's neglecting his duties in the café to play at toy trains. More importantly, she feels–and rightly so–that he is neglecting her too. Clifford knows exactly what he is doing to them both. He wants Roy as his friend, he wants his trains to play with and he doesn't want Hayley to spoil anything for him.

Hayley has to go off to spend time with her sick uncle again, and Roy's left alone with Clifford and the trains. Vera's very disappointed in Roy's behaviour. She tells Roy she thought he was different and now she finds out he is as unreliable as the rest of the blokes that she knows.

Becky Granger crashes in

Hayley starts voluntary work at the local outreach centre, teaching adult literacy to ex–offenders. And it is here that she bumps into Becky, a local menace of the parish. Becky has been in prison for the last three months. and there is violence under her fingernails as, fag in hand and menace in mind, she pesters Hayley, who is too scared to return the following week.

Becky then bursts into Roy's Rolls, demanding that Hayley give her a reference for a job. It is a request that Hayley is too scared to refuse.

Roy runs up the stairs for a pen and some paper as quick as you like, wanting Becky done with and away.

Hayley decides to take a chance on troubled Becky and gives her a job in Roy's Rolls. Roy has to have a word with Becky about chewing while working, although she reckons the mastication helps her concentration. She drops stuff, hits the customers, and changes Roy's radio station to one she prefers. She smacks Les when he badmouths Roy, and she tries to fiddle Tyrone out of a fiver. The factory girls boycott Becky in the café and threaten to take their sandwich order elsewhere, but Hayley insists that everyone deserves a second chance.

Roy and Hayley's unlikely friendship with Becky develops. They even offer to help raise money for Becky to put down the deposit on her own flat. They rifle through some of their old stuff in the attic and come up with items Becky can sell at a car boot sale. Roy finds some first edition *Eagle* comics and a ray gun. They are worth a fortune to a collector, so he is not too happy when he finds out that Becky has taken them to the car boot sale to sell off as junk. However, he breathes a sigh of relief when Becky returns with his goodies in a box after she refused to sell them to a man with sweaty hands. When Roy finally gets an evaluation on the old comics, it comes in at a whopping £1,500.

Slug and The Woody

Becky's mate Slug turns up in the café one day, much to Hayley's disdain. Slug is a scruffy sort in a dirty anorak, with an odd dog on a lead. Roy and Hayley splash the cash on a new, old car. It is a Morris Minor Traveller, more commonly known as a Woody. The Woody, now officially known as Roy and Hayley's pride and joy, goes missing when Slug and Becky take it for a joyride on the moors. Becky is against Slug's idea of taking the car at first, as she doesn't want to upset the Croppers. But Slug persuades her to nick the car with him and off they go, sleeping in the car overnight. When Becky wakes up the next morning, she has an argument with Slug in the car. He drives off, leaving her alone, then abandons the car. When the police ring Roy to say that they have found it, Becky's coat is found on the back seat. Furiously disappointed in Becky for stealing their car, Hayley sacks her and tells her they want nothing more to do with her.

When the police return the Woody to Roy, he hands the car keys to Hayley. He tells the policeman, somewhat proudly:
'My wife's the driver. I prefer to be one of life's passengers'.

Becky tries hard to make amends with Hayley, who is not having any of it. Hayley has been hurt badly and will not let Becky get close to her again. So, when the café goes up in flames and Becky is carried out of the smoke by Lloyd, Roy and Hayley jump to conclusions and reckon Becky set the place on fire out of spite. 'You wretched, wretched woman!' yells Roy to Becky when he sees his livelihood go up in flames. Then Hayley yells at Becky too: 'You nasty, rotten, little cow.'
Despite Becky's protestations, no one believes that she had nothing to do with the fire. So, Hayley has some explaining to do when the fire officer tells her the blaze was started by a fault with the deep fat fryer. Hayley feels even more wracked with guilt with she finally opens the gift that Becky has been trying to give her all week–curtains for the Woody with an embroidered *H* and *R* on them.

Hayley's son Christian

Whey Hayley's Aunty Monica died; Hayley discovered she had an adult son called Christian from a previous relationship when she was still Harold. She hires a private investigator to track Christian down, and eventually introduces herself to him as his aunt. When she trusts herself enough to reveal to Christian that she was once his dad, Christian doesn't take the news well. He lashes out and hits Hayley across the face.

Africa

Deciding a change is as good as rest, Hayley takes up voluntary work in Mozambique for a year. As you would imagine, Roy misses her terribly. At Roy's Rolls there is a Christmas dinner with a difference when Roy invites Becky, Chesney and Kirk to have dinner in the café. Throughout dinner, the phone in the café keeps ringing. It's Hayley, calling from the other side of world, but she seems destined never to speak to her soulmate. Every time Roy tries to answer the phone, something stops him from making the connection with Hayley. But finally, at the end of the dinner when everyone has left, the phone rings and Roy answers. He sits down to wish his beloved a very Merry Christmas.

2008

Roy goes to see Hayley in Africa

Desperate to be near her, Roy flies to Africa to be
with his soulmate, his best friend, his Hayley. There is
only one slight panic on Roy's *To Do* list before he
leaves, as he frets over Becky moving into the flat
above the café while he is away.

When Roy returns from overseas, he takes pity on
Becky living in the hostel and asks her to move into
the flat with him. She is full of cheeky innuendo and
plays Roy up something rotten. She jokes to anyone
who will listen that she is cohabiting with Roy, while
he is at pains to point out that she is simply lodging in
the spare room until Hayley returns. It is an odd
couple relationship between Roy and Becky, yet it is
one that works.
'Guess what I never get?' Becky asks Roy in the café.
'The London Review of Books?' replies Roy, quick
as a flash.

But Roy feels a certain unease at living with Becky. It
is not something he is used to. Roy fits a lock to the
bathroom door and Becky asks Ken for some help in
getting along with Roy.

Following Ken's suggestion, a Scrabble match is set
for Becky and Roy, and Roy waxes lyrical about the
points to be gained from 'XU'.
'Did you know 100 XUs equal a dong?' he asks.

Bats

Bat droppings are spotted by Roy on the new building site on the street. Intrigued, Roy takes the droppings home, examines them on the kitchen table and tells Becky that, as bats are an endangered species, he might have to bring the work on the new flats to a halt.

Tony Gordon talks Jason into smoking out the bats before the woman from *Natural England* calls round. Jason does as he is told, worried that if bats are found then the building site will close down, and he'll be out of a job. When Roy finds out what's gone on, he plans his revenge against Tony. First he tries a sit–in on the site, but he is lifted up and carried away by builders Jason and Bill. Roy then hits on a plan. He gets Ken to drive the Woody to the building site, egged on by Roy in the passenger side and Becky in the back. As Ken steers the car onto the cobbles, Roy tells him where to park it. And when Tony Gordon finds out that the Morris Minor is parked slap bang in front of the building site so that the lorries can't get in, his face will be a joy to behold. It might be a Morris Minor, but it'll give Tony Gordon a Morris Maximum headache.

There is a stand-off on the Street before Tony backs down, after Roy's Ghandi–like passive resistance. Tony donates ten thousand pounds to the bat charity of Roy's choice and Becky gives Roy a power hug in support, something which a sensitive soul like Roy is not yet used to having. His time is spent longing for the nights to fall so he can check his emails from Hayley in Africa.

When Becky starts seeing married man Jason Grimshaw, it is a relationship which Roy does not approve of. Becky storms out of the café, the flat and Roy's life after he tells her she has the morals of a stray cat. Becky replies with some choice words of her own, which cut deep. She calls Roy a weirdo. Ouch. And she calls Hayley a weirdo too. Double ouch. Roy's so upset with this turn of events that he hyperventilates into rubber gloves, and Becky moves into Eileen's.

Hayley returns from Africa

But there is some good news in Roy's Rolls. Roy takes a phone call from Hayley to say she is coming home from abroad. Roy prepares for the return of Hayley from foreign shores and ponders buying her some new bubble bath.

Wearing his best shirt with anticipation, Roy gathers a small crowd in the café for Hayley's return. But she is quiet, is Hayley, after a year away from the Street, and does not have much to say for herself. As she tries to adjust to life back in the flat, Hayley's gob smacked to find her husband checking over Becky's make–up before Becky hits the town in a short spangly frock. She is even more lost for words when Becky shouts 'Laters!' as she heads out of the door, only for Roy to respond with the same. By 'eck, there have been some changes made while Hayley has been gone.

Hayley has trouble settling in. She tells Roy she wants to go back to Africa, and while that is very hard for him to hear, he realises that if that is what she wants, then he has to let her go. But then she tells him the truth–it is not Africa her heart yearns for, but Olaf the team leader, who she had a crush on. Once it has been admitted, Hayley feels ashamed, and Roy forgives her everything. There are big hugs all round and Hayley decides to stay.

She heads to the factory, where Tony Gordon wants Hayley as Supervisor, but Hayley wants to do something more meaningful instead. Roy suggests she talks to Emily about volunteering with the youth centre.

Over at Roy's Rolls, Hayley and Roy open up on Christmas Day to feed the homeless of Weatherfield with a determined grins and plenty of gravy. Hayley reckons it will be the best thing to happen to her at Christmas, apart from getting a kiss from Roy under the mistletoe. Roy blushes when he hears this.

2009

Anna starts work at Roy's Rolls

In Roy's Rolls, Anna Windass starts work, serving up
the barm cakes. She does a good job and throws out
Theresa Morton who turns up drunk. Roy decides he
can trust Anna, enough to give her his customer
number for Priceco (73542553) along with his
password (PuffingBilly). Feckless Eddie Windass
steals both the number and password and spends a
fortune on booze, for which Roy will be charged and
Anna will be blamed.

But as Eddie tries to leave through the security exit at
Priceco, the buzzers go off and the store is put on
alert. The store manager tells Eddie that he has won a
European weekend break to a destination of his
choice. Roy finds out about this, of course, and has a
showdown with Eddie for stealing his Priceco
identity. Hayley finds out what has happened when
she goes to Priceco and finds life–size cardboard
cutouts of Eddie posing as 'Roy Cropper–our
millionth customer' and the proud winner of a
European weekend city break for two. Roy bars
Eddie from the café but tells Anna she can keep her
job as long as Eddie pays the cash back. Roy even
prepares a repayment schedule for Eddie, although he
doesn't hold out much hope of getting the money
back soon.

Tony Gordon

After Roy's run–in with Tony Gordon over the bat
problem in the building site for the new flats, Tony

seeks his revenge on Roy. He chooses his moment as Hayley's upstairs in the flat on her own and Roy's out bat watching by the canal with just a torch and a notebook. Tony follows Roy down to the canal, and when he finds him, there's a scuffle between the two men. Roy's notebook and torch go flying, and as Roy hovers at the water's edge after the tussle with Tony, he pleads with him.

'But I can't swim!' he cries.

'Good,' Tony Gordon replies, before letting Roy fall backwards into the murky depths with only his shopping bag to keep him afloat. Tony starts to run away, but suddenly stops, turns and runs back. Not only does he run back, but he also rescues Roy, saves his life and gives him the kiss of life. Roy recovers, and psycho–Tony turns himself in at Weatherfield police station.

2010

Roy and Hayley have much on their mind when Roy makes a list and undertakes a life and death audit. He decides that he and Hayley need to be legally wed, in case one of them dies. You might remember they were 'wed' back in 1999, but the law has now changed to allow transsexuals to legally marry. Hayley takes Roy's news to mean he's proposing to her again, and she gets excited about a big wedding and a new frock. Roy just wants the legal aspects taken care of, and when Hayley starts planning and wanting a big wedding, he takes back his marriage proposal. The Croppers are now at odds over their future. Hayley wants a wedding, while Roy just wants things legal, tidy and right. Why can't they have both? For now, it seems they can't agree to disagree, and they fall out over something as trivial as Hayley's new salsa dress.

Hayley's held hostage

When Tony Gordon breaks out of jail with the help of his cellmate Robbie, he storms back to the Street and into Underworld. With murder on his mind, he puts a gun to Carla Connor's pretty head. He tapes Carla's mouth shut and ties her to the factory's executive swivel chair. Oh, he's a bad 'un and no mistake. And then he does the same to Hayley, on the cheaper chair, and with the two women taped up and tied down, terrible Tony throws petrol around after shooting Robbie dead on the factory floor.

Hayley manages to wiggle free, and Tony throws her out onto the cobbles as the cops buzz outside and a crowd gathers to find out what is going on. Carla wiggles herself free too and makes a run for the door as Tony sets light to the petrol and Underworld goes up in flames. Carla runs out and Tony runs after her, but then he turns and walks back into the inferno, never to be seen again.

Wedding No. 2 – August 30, 2010

After he has taken back his proposal of marriage, Roy tries again and proposes once more to Hayley, upstairs in their flat. Hayley accepts and breaks the news to the factory girls over cakes in Roy's Rolls. 'We're getting married!' she yells excitedly.
To which everyone replies, 'We thought you already were.'
Well, no, they never were, not properly and legally, but with a change in the law for transsexuals to marry, they can now be legally wed. 'Do they sell a card in The Kabin for that?' asks Deirdre when she finds out the news.

Mary takes it upon herself to start planning Hayley's wedding, although it is clear this is something that Hayley is not totally comfortable with, especially when Mary hands Hayley her own marriage portfolio, the dossier she has been working on for years. It contains details of everything from dresses and tiaras to garters and cakes. Mary has clearly been planning her own wedding for some time, hoping for something old (Norris) something new (the motorhome), something borrowed (Tina's job at the Kabin) and something blue (Rita's exotic dancing past).

Mary takes Hayley on a day out to look at wedding venues. She organises the day and prepares an itinerary and maps. With Dolly Parton on the CD in the motorhome, Mary drives Hayley out to a country hall. Hayley is too polite to say much to Mary, but it is clear she is uncomfortable with being involved in Mary's manic world of marriage. That is, until Hayley spots a steam train running alongside the wedding hall and knows immediately that Roy would love to have it included as part of their big day.

Hayley's hen party starts off in the Rovers, with the girls dressed up in sexy nurse outfits. Mary is upset, as she has not been invited, so she leaves the girls to their debauchery and heads home for a fish supper. The party moves on from the Rovers to the café, where there is a Latin lothario waiting to whisk Hayley around the café floor with some sexy salsa moves. Roy even dons a rakish moustache and has a smile on his face as he joins in with the hen party fun.

But Roy is smiling even more on his wedding day when he gets the chance to drive a steam train–a Lancashire Fusilier No. 44871–to their wedding venue. As Roy and Chesney chuff it out up front in the engine room, the guests are enjoying themselves and having fun in the first-class carriage. At the end of the train are Hayley and the bridesmaids, Becky and Fiz, unaware that Mary is intent on derailing Roy and Hayley's big day. Mary has only gone and uncoupled Hayley's carriage from the main train! And so, Hayley's carriage sits on a train line in the middle of nowhere until they figure out what has happened and then the girls get out. At first they walk, then run, then find a pump wagon. Hayley lifts up her wedding dress as Becky and Fiz give it what–for on the pump wagon to get the bride to the venue in time for her to say, 'I do'.

In his wedding speech, Roy makes reference to the change in the law which allows their wedding to be recognised legally this time around.

'It is eleven years since we last registered to be married and we were informed that we could not,' he says. 'We have remained still, and the world has turned to meet *us*. My message to you, Hayley, is this–the world can change its rules, its laws and its opinions as frequently as it chooses, but I will remain standing beside you. That will not change.'

2011

Roy's mum Sylvia arrives

When Roy's mum Sylvia turns up to see her son, she comes into the café and looks around in distaste and her first words are, 'I knew this was a bad idea.' Well, it goes from bad to worse when she finds out that her boy Roy is now a married man, and he hadn't breathed a word to his own mother about it. When she finds out about Hayley's past, she is stunned and silenced but softly and gently warms to Hayley in time.

Sylvia has returned to Roy's life after attending the funeral of Roy's stepdad. Roy did not go to the funeral, as he did not want anything to do with his stepdad. But it doesn't look like he has a choice about wanting anything to do with his mum. She immediately gets her feet under the table at Roy's Rolls café. She also gets her mighty frame behind the counter when she helps out a frantic Roy, who is having a busy day and needs a spare pair of hands to help out.
'Hmm … you don't look like the salad type,' Sylvia muses to Tyrone when he pops in for a pie and chips.

Hayley offers her mum–in–law a lift back to her nursing home, and although Sylvia is not too keen on getting into the Woody– 'It looks like summat you wind up!'–she gets in, and Hayley drives her home. However, the nursing home is rather down-at-heel and not the sort of place you would want a relative to live in, if you had a say in such things. Hayley alerts Roy to this when she gets back home.

Sylvia starts helping out in Roy's Rolls, adding her tuppence of insight to every conversation she eavesdrops on. 'I know all about women like Tracy Barlow,' she tells Becky. 'I was almost one myself.'

Sylvia soon starts showing some chinks in her armour when she softens and has a bit of a moment alone in the café. She takes a photo of Roy as a child out of her bag and sighs softly over it. Sylvia and Roy start slowly building bridges and making amends for years of neglecting each other.

Sylvia decides to shake things up at Roy's Rolls and take charge and charge she does. She charges for use of the ketchup, the salt, the pepper and the loo. The customers are up in arms complaining, but it is water off a duck's back to Sylvia. She is intent on pushing up the profits, and woe betide anyone who gets in her way. And that person is Norris, who nicks the key to the loo, demanding his right to a free pee. Well, Sylvia spots him and locks him in there overnight. Oh dear, what can the matter be? Norris Cole is locked in the lavatory. He's there from Friday to Monday and nobody knows he's there. Except Sylvia does you see.

Mary starts fretting about Norris' whereabouts, convinced he has been kidnapped. And just when Mary starts wondering which one of the Suchet brothers will play Norris in the film of his life, Sylvia unlocks the door to the lavvy and Norris is free. Mary is not best pleased and calls a council of war with Emily and Dennis to demand that Norris is given compensation for his night in the netty. It is agreed that Norris, Mary, Emily and Dennis will be given a slap–up banquet at Roy's Rolls and that Sylvia will play waitress, as an apology for her behaviour. But as Sylvia serves up the food for them all at the meal, she does not and will not say the word *sorry*. She does give a wry smile to Dennis, though; it is clear she has got her eye on him.

Sylvia continues to help out at Roy's Rolls and is over the moon when she finds out she has won a cruise in a competition. But it's a competition she entered using a slogan that Mary had written. Mary, as you can imagine, is not happy with Sylvia's behaviour once again. Roy refuses to be drawn into the fight, but he makes it clear to his mother that he is not happy with her too. However, this does not deter Sylvia from swanning off on her sea cruise. When she returns, Sylvia is full of tales of a sprightly, elderly gentleman called Milton, an American, who gave her the glad eye while she was onboard. And it is not long before Milton arrives from overseas to see Sylvia.

2012

Milton

Milton has got an eye for business and in Roy's Rolls, he eyes up the till rolls and spots a little goldmine. He suggests that he and Roy go into partnership to open a string of railway–themed restaurants called *Beef Encounter*. But not even Milton's fancy–pants computer presentation, complete with steam train noises and the suggestion that staff could dress up as signalmen, can turn Roy's head. He turns Milton's offer down flat, much to Sylvia's chagrin. Roy choo–choo–chooses to run Roy's Rolls just as he has always done.

Roy's not happy when Sylvia supports Milton's plan of opening the *Beef Encounter* restaurants. But Sylvia remembers the help and support Roy and Hayley have shown her over the last few months and knows she can't go along with Milton and his daft plan.

Milton has turned Sylvia's head, and she prepares to leave and swap the Street for the States when Milton offers to whisk her away, away, away down South to Dixie.
'I have a first-class ticket for a first-class dame,' Milton croons to Sylvia.
It is enough to turn Sylvia's head–a little, anyway. She breaks the news to Roy that she intends to leave. She hopes desperately that he will say he does not want her to go, but Roy keeps quiet, even though he is, in fact, hoping that she will stay.
'Just say the word and I will stay,' Sylvia says.
But the word remains unsaid. And so, Sylvia leaves,

although it is not what either mum or son want. She leaves and she goes without a hug or a hold, just a handshake from Roy. And then she comes right back! 'I can't be doing with faucets and closets and pants, not at my age,' she moans. Roy is happy, Sylvia is happy and the good ship Roy's Rolls gets back on an even keel.

As Sylvia settles back into the Croppers' lives, Hayley gets hyped up about going ballroom dancing. Mary, on finding out about Hayley's dancing class, drags Norris along after she finds out he once danced with Vera Duckworth in Blackpool's tower ballroom. Well, he says he danced, but I think we all remember him best for that very, very long slide along the floor on his knees.

Mad Mary

Norris can't dance with Mary, though. He says she has got two left feet, and calls her dancing 'deranged', although Mary says she is 'animated' and so Norris drops Mary as his dance partner and takes up with Hayley instead. Kitted out in fascinator and frock, Hayley glides across the dance floor with Norris as her guide, while back home in the café, Roy challenges Mary to a game of chess. It soon transpires that Mary has more on her mind than castles and knights and wants to lead Roy a merry dance of her own, as she determines to make Norris jealous by flirting with Roy.

As Hayley and Norris go to the dance class again, Mary brings her chess set once more to Roy's Rolls. Mary's friendship with Roy is upsetting Hayley somewhat, but Roy seems oblivious to the attention Mary is giving him–for now, anyway. It is not long before Mary shows her true colours and starts lusting after Roy. She cries in the café over Roy's choice of music, classical Elgar. She cries over losing her father. Roy hands her a tea towel for her to dry her tears with. She blows her nose on it and hands it back. Over their game of chess in the café while Hayley is out dancing, Mary talks of how she could have worn a low-cut blouse to distract Roy's attention. She giggles like a schoolgirl while eating her sandwiches with Roy. 'Oh, I've dropped some piccalilli on your bishop.'

Mary gets her talons further into Roy when Hayley is called away to look after her Uncle Bert, who has taken ill once again. With Hayley away, Mary invites Roy to accompany her to a musical event. 'I've never been so moved by a wind section,' she says, giggling like a girl later in the café when Roy invites her in for a cocoa.

Mary even starts to help out in Roy's Rolls. Roy is on his own and grateful for her help, but she pushes him further than he wants to go with their friendship. She invites Roy to an Elgar concert in another town and Roy agrees to go with her, although it means an overnight stay. But while Mary dreams of a romantic musical getaway, Roy puts paid to her plan. He tells her that while she has only booked two rooms in the hotel, he has booked three concert tickets, as Hayley will be joining them too. But in a mix–up with the hotel booking, there are no rooms left and Mary invites Roy to hunker down in the motorhome with her. Roy, already fretting that he is missing Hayley's dancing competition, demands to return home. Mary drives home disappointed. It is clear she has a crush on Mr. Cropper the size of Salford itself.

Mary's attention to Roy has not passed Hayley by, and she demands to know what Mary is up to. At first Mary denies everything but then she comes clean and admits she has been after Roy for quite some time. 'But men I like don't like me. And men I don't like me,' sighs Mary.
Well, Roy, as we all know, only has eyes for Hayley.

After Hayley has a word with Mary, and Anna gives Mary the evil eye in the café for giving Roy the glad eye, Mary decides to leave Weatherfield. She breaks the news to Norris, who is surprised, shaken and stirred. He stammers:
'But there's people round here's as'll miss yer!'
Mary raises an eyebrow and hopes to hear the answer she needs, but all Norris will say in return to the eyebrow is, 'Like … Roy… and Emily.'
Norris is quite clearly perturbed at the news that Mary might be leaving and so rushes round to Roy and Hayley to tell them the news. Norris hopes that Roy and Hayley can stop Mary from moving away in her motorhome and indeed, they do. Hayley has a heart-to-heart in the motorhome with Mary. She tells her gently but firmly to leave Roy alone and that they want her to stay. Mary agrees, and Norris is overjoyed to hear Mary has decided to stay. But has he ever told her that? Has he 'eck as like.

Mary shows her gratitude to the Croppers when she gives them two transatlantic flight tickets she has won in one of the many competitions she enters. She hands both tickets to the Croppers after she overhears them talking about Roy's mum Sylvia, who is in Palm Springs with Milton. Mary insists that Roy and Hayley use the tickets to visit Sylvia there.

While the Croppers are away, Mary looks after Roy's Rolls and opens it up in the evenings. She sets up a Spanish theme night–Café Olé–serving tapas and gazpacho. Nick's not happy that Mary's opened the café on an evening, putting it in direct competition with The Bistro. Oh, Roy will not be happy when he comes back.

Mary holds more theme nights in the café, but after the Moroccan night, Anna tells Mary she is quitting. She says the theme nights are too much hard work, and she is not sure Roy would be happy if he knew. Mary brings in Norris to work on the French theme night and even opens up the Croppers' flat to accommodate more diners. Oh Mary. Oh dear. When Roy finds out he won't be happy at all, even if the theme nights are a financial success. It is not what Roy and Hayley are about, and Roy will not want to upset the workers at The Bistro, which is what Mary has gone and done. Takings at The Bistro have hit rock bottom since Mary's theme nights have begun.

2013

Sylvia returns

When Roy and Hayley return from Palm Springs, Roy doesn't want Mary back to help him in the café. No one blames Roy for sacking Mary after she almost lost him his licence by selling alcohol at her theme nights.

The Croppers have more on their minds when Sylvia waltzes back into Roy's Rolls from America with her suitcase and some secrets. She tells a stunned Roy, who is somewhat surprised to see his mum:
'Don't just stand there with your sausage in your hand!'
And then a trunk arrives with all her belongings in it, sent over from Milton in Palm Springs. 'We used to have a trunk just like that when I was little,' notes Roy, to which Sylvia replies, 'Yes, you used to play with your little Dinkys in it.'
We then see Sylvia on the phone to Milton in the States, and it is clear that things are over between them, but she has not yet told Roy. She has also not told him that she is skint and pretends her purse has been lost in town.

Sylvia continues being secretive and lies to Roy that she has lost her watch. She also refuses to tell him why she gets dolled up to the nines when she goes out for the day. Roy knows something is up but is not sure what, just yet. It all falls into place when Roy asks Lloyd to reveal where his Streetcars cab dropped Sylvia off in town. Roy is shocked to discover that Sylvia has gone to the Canalside Road Casino. Roy sneaks into the casino to find Sylvia on the slot machines.

Sylvia comes clean to Roy and admits that she has a gambling addiction. The real reason she is skint, she tells Roy, is because she has lost over £2,000 on casino slots. So, when Roy displays his passion for numbers and counting in the café, Sylvia hits on a plan.

'You're my Rain Man!' she screams, and her eyes light up.

Roy ropes in Dennis and Ken and proceeds to knuckle down and cash in on a casino game of blackjack by counting the cards to increase his winning odds. And win he does, enough to give Sylvia her £2,000 back and for Roy to walk out of the casino and away from gambling with his head held high. But Sylvia wants more and begs Roy to return to play again and win more.

'You're as bad as Alec Gilroy!' he spits at her in the café before walking out.

Those of us with long memories will recall that Alec Gilroy spotted in Roy the potential to make money out of his memory skills as a novelty turn. And Roy, being Roy, turned Alec down flat.

Roy's dad

Sylvia receives a surprise phone call from an old friend called Dorothy, who lives in a care home. Dorothy has found an unopened letter from December 2011, addressed to Sylvia. Sylvia opens the letter and tells Hayley it is from Roy's dad, St. John. Hayley can't understand why Sylvia lies to Roy about the letter, and she begs Sylvia to let Roy read the letter, to give him some closure about his dad.

'Don't you go all middle–class words on me!' Sylvia warns her daughter–in–law.

Hayley convinces Sylvia to let Roy read the letter, and he decides to go in search of his dad.

Sadly, for Roy, his search reveals that St. John died a few months earlier. Roy tries, and fails miserably, to cope with the fact that the dad he went looking for no longer exists.

'I was contented,' he tells Hayley, before she made him read the letter and encouraged him to seek out his dad. 'And I'm no longer contented, not now.'

Hayley can only apologise, or at least try to.

'I'm truly sorry, Roy, if I'm in any way to blame …' to which Roy silences her with 'But you are, Hayley. You *are*. You are to blame.'

A visit to St. John's grave does little to ease Roy's mind, although playing with his childhood toy trains helps it back on the right track.

Roy takes the news of his dad's death very badly. He internalises his grief and starts shining up everything in the café that needs shining and some things that don't. He is polishing stuff that has had the life polished out of it already. Once that is all done, he takes to sweeping the Street and ticking off young Craig for littering the cobbles. Hayley keeps harping on to her husband, but Sylvia warns her to leave well alone, as she knows Roy too well.

As Roy tries to cope with the enormity of his dad's death, there are strange goings–on in the café. Roy wakes one morning to find the condiments all lined up in size order. He swears to Hayley that he did not do it, and he wonders who did. Sylvia and Hayley laugh about poltergeists, and Beth jokes about having an app on her phone that finds ectoplasm. Could it be Roy's disturbed mind, sleepwalking and sleep–sorting, and he can't remember what he has done the next day?

The strange goings–on continue and things move about in the night, mainly Roy and his wandering, disturbed mind. But Roy is convinced there is an intruder who is breaking in and tidying up. He stays up all night with a flask and a torch, determined to catch the nocturnal nuisance.

When this does not work, Roy sets up CCTV in the café to determine who is breaking in. No one is, of course–it is Roy with his restless mind who has been moving things around after hours. But the CCTV does capture images of Roy piling the chairs up on a table in the café, then leaving through the front door and wandering outside in his pyjamas. He is sleepwalking, and Deirdre finds him in his dressing gown on the Red Rec as she is out walking Eccles. Deirdre gets Roy back home safe and sound, in body if not in mind. Sylvia and Hayley try to talk some sense into Roy, but he will not listen and be helped–not yet anyway. Sylvia insists that her son needs some professional help and begs him to talk to Hayley.

Roy finally opens up to Hayley and talks about the turmoil he is in that has led him to go sleepwalking in the night and almost setting the café on fire. Hayley gets Roy to visit his GP, but just before the receptionist calls Roy's name for his appointment, he is gone. Hayley drags him back in. The GP tells Roy that he has to spend a night in a sleep clinic to get to the root of the problem and in the meantime to try meditation, not medication. Sylvia huffs and puffs at the notion of this.

'You might as well hug a tree,' she declares. 'Or rub on some essential oil of ramalamadingdong.'

Cancer

As Roy improves and settles in body and mind, Hayley visits her GP for a reason of her own. She has blood tests taken which come back needing more investigation and is very soon sent to have an ultrasound too. Hayley is beside herself with worry over what could be wrong, and while she does her best to hide this from Roy, Sylvia's sharper and notices something is up. Hayley has got no choice but to tell her. There is a blockage in her bile duct which could be cancer.

Hayley's worst fears are confirmed when she is diagnosed with pancreatic cancer. Roy takes refuge in research online, demanding that Hayley eats organic broccoli to beat the free radicals. Roy's insistence on trying to wrap Hayley up in cotton wool gets right on Hayley's nerves. He has got Hayley's welfare at heart but takes it too far.

One night he follows Hayley into The Bistro, where she is celebrating Audrey's birthday with a drink of bubbly, grabs the glass from her hand and tells her not to drink. He announces loudly to everyone in The Bistro who will listen (and most of them do):
'You are gravely ill, and you could die!'
It is too much for Hayley and she gives Roy a stern

talking-to before storming off home.

News of Hayley's cancer grows on the gossip grapevine, and when Tracy tells Roy she is sorry to hear the news, Roy gives her short shrift. In a wonderful speech, Roy reminds Tracy of the stress and the anguish she has caused the Croppers over the years. Let us not forget she drove Roy to consider suicide over baby Patience/Amy. Roy blames Tracy for the stress that might have led to Hayley's cancer, to which Tracy spits back that it is more likely Hayley's hormone pills that have caused it.
Protective of Roy once again, Fiz stands up and yells at Tracy to leave Roy alone. He makes his way back to the flat and to Hayley, where it does not take long for the two of them to make up over a cup of tea and a plate of cheese on toast. Roy holds Hayley and Hayley holds Roy. He tells her she has given him the happiest time of his life, and Hayley tells her husband: 'I don't want to go. I always thought the best was yet to come for us both.'

Knowing that her time is limited as the cancer worsens, Hayley wants Roy to learn how to drive. She wants him prepared as best as he can be for when she is no longer around to drive him about. But Roy gets dropped by the driving instructor for driving too slowly and being too pedantic on the road. Undeterred, Hayley rings Dave's School of Motoring and arranges another instructor to take Roy out on the road in the Woody.

Christian again

79

Hayley decides to contact her son Christian, although Roy doesn't think it is such a good idea. The last time Christian was in their lives, he attacked Hayley when she revealed to Christian she had once been his dad, Harold. But Hayley is determined and wants very much to meet Christian again. It does not bode well when Christian turns up at Roy's Rolls after Hayley contacts him out of the blue and asks to meet up. They retire to the Rovers, but Christian still has trouble with the fact that Hayley is a transsexual. Christian is now a dad to two kids of his own, and Hayley tells him to 'to be a good dad'.

'I couldn't be worse than you,' he replies.

Hayley takes her cue, and with Roy beside her, walks out of the pub and out of her son's life. Back at the flat, Hayley encourages Roy to continue his driving lessons and to plan for his life when there is a great big Hayley–shaped hole in it.

Blackpool

Deciding to make the most of the time she has left, Hayley tells Roy she wants to go to Blackpool. Roy plans their time to perfection, with an itinerary in one hand– 'At 4.30 p.m. I have scheduled in some time for spontaneity'– and a candyfloss in the other. The two of them walk along the prom with a stuffed elephant in Roy's bag that he has won on the slots for Hayley. The pair of them go for a paddle in the sea and then Hayley drags Roy into a fortune-telling booth. The clairvoyant sees trouble in the tarot cards but hides it from the Croppers. When she hears that Hayley would have loved to have danced in the tower ballroom, but it is closed for maintenance, she hits on a plan. The fortune-teller tells Hayley and Roy to return to the ballroom and divines that Hayley will dance. Roy thinks it is all a load of cobblers, but to his surprise, the ballroom is open when they return, and the pair of them foxtrot around the floor to the mighty Wurlitzer.

'Thanks, mother!' yells the tower ballroom manager to his mum up in the balcony, who turns out to be the fortune-teller herself.

Hayley's right to die

Back home in Weatherfield after their Blackpool trip, Hayley has news for Roy. She tells him that she wants to choose when she dies. She does not want to let the cancer dictate when she goes. Roy cannot understand this, not one bit, and they argue and row, with Hayley walking out. She moves in with Fiz and Tyrone, but she collapses and is rushed to hospital, where she is treated for infection. It brings Roy to his senses and immediately to Hayley's bedside, where the two of them make up after rowing over Hayley's right to die when she chooses. But it is an issue that is not settled yet between them. It is just not being talked about, not while Hayley recovers in her hospital bed.

Hayley returns home from hospital just as Roy finishes off decorating their bedroom with the most hideous wallpaper Hayley's ever seen. Things are still strained between them, with Roy unable to accept the fact that Hayley wants to end her own life. And Hayley is unable to accept that Roy refuses to see things her way.

'I want to die as Hayley!' she says, terrified of losing her mind as she nears the end and reverting to thinking she is Harold again. 'I've been there, done that, worn the Y–fronts!' she yells at Roy, who is still unable to cope.

Hayley's cancer and asserting her right to die is causing all kinds of misery for Roy, and he really has trouble coping with it all. The only way he knows how to cope is to put Hayley's wishes ahead of his own. It is the only thing that Roy knows how to do.

As Hayley's health deteriorates and her relationship with Roy suffers, she takes on the task of designing and creating Carla Connor's wedding dress. Hayley is overjoyed to have been asked to make Carla's dress, but Roy worries Hayley is taking on too big a job in the state that she is in.

Undeterred, Hayley cracks on with designing Carla's dress. The design she shows Carla is a dress with puffed sleeves and frills, and Carla's not happy. She is not, after all, a puffed-sleeves-and-frills sort of girl. Moaning to Peter in the factory, Carla wonders if asking Hayley to design her wedding dress was a good idea after all.
'I've just asked a terminally ill woman with no sense of style to design my wedding dress. Do I walk down the aisle looking like a sack of spuds, or shatter her dreams, break her heart and sack her?'
So, it is back to the drawing board for Hayley as Carla rips up her design and sticks bits of paper together, matching bits from one frock design with another. Carla shows Hayley her proposed design.
'Can you make it?' she asks Hayley.
'Yes, I can!' Hayley replies, fired up.

Hayley's first chemotherapy session makes her decisive. She drags Roy to visit a funeral director, as she wants to start planning her funeral. Roy's not happy to be taken along without knowing what Hayley is doing, and it is so sad to see the Croppers bickering, but totally understandable too. Roy finally comes around to Hayley's way of thinking and they start researching humanist funerals online. In between choosing caskets, Hayley puts the finishing touches to Carla's wedding dress and takes it into the factory for Carla to see.

'Do you like it?' asks Hayley.

'No, I don't like it,' Carla replies. 'I don't like it one bit. I love it!'

Christian returns

Hayley's son Christian turns up again, but this time Fiz gets to him first, warning him to back off, and tells him that Hayley has cancer. But Christian does not back off; he returns once more with a plea for Hayley to give him £5,000 and in return she can see her grandchildren. Does she fall for the sorry sob story from her son? Yes, I'm afraid she does. Roy cannot understand his wife's decision. Fiz and Ches cannot understand it either. Hayley tells them all in the Rovers that she has had the best day ever after meeting her grandkids and she doesn't begrudge Christian the cash, not one bit.

Devastating news

Hayley is given devastating news. The consultant at the hospital tells Hayley and Roy that Hayley has only weeks to live. A scan at the hospital shows the cancer has spread to her liver, the chemotherapy isn't working, and no alternative course of treatment can be used to save her.

So far, Hayley has been stoic, she has been upbeat, but finally she breaks down in spectacular style, and who can blame her?
'It is not fair,' she cries to Roy. 'I'm not ready!'
The Croppers return to the flat from the hospital and Hayley is angry, very angry, and throws their Christmas tree to the floor. When she has calmed down later, sitting on the sofa with Roy, he tells his wife how much he loves her and how much she means to him.
'You have turned an apology of an existence into a life.'

2014

Hayley's final goodbye

Hayley's news that she has only weeks to live filters around the Street after she and Roy agree that friends should be told. Roy takes his shopping bag and goes to break the news to Carla. Carla demands to see Hayley, barges into her bedroom and gets into bed with her for a cosy little chat.

As Hayley deteriorates she loses her appetite, and the only thing she can stomach is strawberries. Roy is desperate to buy as many strawberries for Hayley as he can, but when he gets to the deli there are none to be found. Roy harangues the poor deli manager, determined to get strawberries for Hayley, whatever the price or the cost. Fortunately, Fiz finds some, but they will not scan at the till, as they have passed their 'best before' date. The strawberry saga is too much for Roy. He knows he has to have them for Hayley. He rips the punnet from the checkout operator's hand and heads out of the deli door, but slips as he does so, landing on his bum, and the strawberries go flying all over the place. He tells Hayley the truth when he returns home, and she's angry at first but soon sees the funny side.

Hayley is in a great deal of increasing pain and has her painkillers increased, but she's slipping away in front of Roy's eyes. Hayley reminds Roy that she is set on taking her own life when she feels the time is right.

'When?' he whispers, not ready to hear her answer. 'Not today,' she replies. 'Probably not tomorrow. But soon.'

Strawberries remain the only thing that Hayley feels well and able enough to eat. But her request for strawberries brings more than she bargained for. Kirk and Tyrone drive to the strawberry farm to collect strawberries for her. But the problem is, they can't just buy a punnet from the farm, so they end up with a vanload. And after Hayley's eaten what she can, Roy's café turns into a strawberry jam–making production line. Hayley is grateful for the strawberries, the jam, the love and the care her friends have taken in preparing it all for her.

Hayley is now frail, unable to walk far as her pain and exhaustion increase. She tells Roy she feels the time is now right for her to go and she wants to start saying her goodbyes. Roy wheels Hayley down the cobbles in her wheelchair. She says her goodbyes to Chesney and Sinead on the Street and to Carla in the factory. When she spots Tracy Barlow she gives a well–deserved farewell to the woman who has caused the Croppers so much pain and anguish over the years. Hayley tells Tracy:
'Your mother's ashamed of you, your daughter barely knows who you are, and your donor kidney would have left you if it could.'

It is now time for Hayley to go. It is time. She tells Roy that she wants to end her own life on her own terms before the pain becomes too much and before her mind reverts to life before she became Hayley. She wants to go when the time is right for her.

'My body's shutting down and my mind's not far behind it.'

'When?' Roy asks her, not daring to hear what she might say.

'Tomorrow,' she replies.

The January day dawns when Hayley plans to take her own life. Roy begs her to reconsider, but she will not. She sends him to the Kabin on an errand, and while he is out, she irons his best shirt for him to wear after she has gone. Hayley wants him well dressed on her funeral day. Roy notices the shirt hanging crisp and fresh from a coat hanger when he returns from the shop. But his mind is too busy with the enormity of what Hayley is about to do to take much else in. He tries again to get Hayley to change her mind. With tears in his eyes, he begs her not to do it, but Hayley is insistent, determined. Her mind has been made up for some time.

'I said it was today and I meant it,' she tells Roy.

'Sorry. Waiting's just making this harder.'

'You have freedom of choice. I beg you to exercise it,' he says.

But Hayley refuses to change her mind.

'I'm ready,' she says.

Roy replies, sadly: 'I'm not.'

Hayley leans on Roy as he takes her into their bedroom. As they sit together on their bed, Hayley holds Roy's hands as she tells him that his life must continue without her.

'I don't know how I'll go on,' he cries.

Hayley replies: 'You'll be my eyes and my ears, my heart for years to come. Promise me that. I don't care about your science and your logic. Some things just

don't stop–and you and me are one of them.'
Hayley raises her prepared lethal cocktail of drugs to
her lips, but before she takes her first sip, she tells
Roy that he must not, under any circumstances, touch
the glass or her medication. The suicide which is the
release from her pain has to be hers alone; she does
not want Roy implicated in any way.
'I'm so glad I knew you, Roy. Thank you.'
'I ... I... I'm the one who should be grateful,' he
replies.
Hayley continues, 'I'd not swap the few years we had
for a thousand of anyone else's. 'Cos I know what it is
to be loved, truly loved.'
'Always,' says Roy, with tears in his eyes.
'Then remember it,' Hayley tells him. 'I love you.
Always have. Always will. I'm so sorry I have to go.'

And with that, Roy is alone, lying on the bed next to
the body of his beloved Hayley. Hayley's pain has
now left her and is over. Without Hayley in his life,
the agony for Roy is just about to begin.

The perfect duet

Reeling from Hayley's suicide, her funeral proves
almost too hard for Roy to bear. At the humanist
service, Fiz gives a reading, saying how caring
Hayley was and how she always put others first. The
words stir emotion in Roy that he had kept hidden so
far from the others. He interrupts Fiz's speech.
'People deserve to know the truth,' he says, standing
up to address the gathered crowd. 'I'm sorry, but they
do.'

It looks as if Roy is about to reveal Hayley's suicide

to everyone at her funeral. He continues, 'The truth …
the truth is, she was not perfect. She was flawed. She
was real. She was my light, my beautiful coruscating
light. My life was a dark corner, and she came into it.
I could see. I could see the world with her. I
understood life. I understood love. She was my
constant, my comfort, my compass. Hayley was my
truth, without her, I … ' and then he faltered and
could speak no more.

Tyrone helps Roy back to his seat and the celebrant
continues with the service, announcing the music
Hayley has chosen for her final farewell. It is the
second movement from Bach's Double Violin
Concerto. Hayley had specially requested this, the
celebrant announces, because Roy had once told her it
was 'the perfect duet'.

After the services, the wake is held in the Rovers
where Carla raises a toast to Hayley. Roy is
uncomfortable with the attention and suffocated by
the sympathy of the mourners in the pub. He takes
himself to a quiet corner on his own as Hayley's
friends and colleagues drink to her memory. Sean
puts one of Hayley's favourite songs on the jukebox
and everyone sings along, but not Roy. He leaves the
Rovers quietly, unnoticed. With his shopping bag in
his hand, Roy walks out onto the cold Weatherfield
Streets, in despair and alone.

About the author

Glenda Young is a lifelong Coronation Street fan. She is editor of the Coronation Street Blog at coronationstreetupdates.blogspot.com and Corrie.net, the world's first and original Coronation Stret fan site.

Her bestselling sagas are set in a northeast mining village in 1919, and her cosy crimes are set in modern-day Scarborough. The crime series was shortlisted for Best New Crime Series with Val McDermid and Richard Osman in the Dead Good Readers Awards.

Glenda is published by Headline. She has also written TV tie-in books for ITV's *Coronation Street* and is an award-winning short story writer.

She was one of six finalists in the coveted Clement & Le Frenais comedy award.

Glenda also has a unique claim to fame, she's the writer of *Riverside*, a weekly soap opera published in The People's Friend magazine since 2016.

Glenda's website: http://glendayoungbooks.com

X and Instagram: http://www.twitter.com/flaming_nora

Facebook http://www.facebook.com/GlendaYoungAuthor

Printed in Dunstable, United Kingdom